WHETHER YOU WANT TO HELP A FRIEND, CLASSMATE, YOURSELF, OR JUST LEARN MORE, THIS GUIDE IS FOR YOU.

BUT FIRST, REVIEW THE BULLYING BASICS. YOU MAY ALREADY KNOW A LOT ABOUT THE TOPIC, BUT SOME THINGS MAY SURPRISE YOU.

ARE YOU IN KINDERGARTEN, FIRST GRADE, OR SECOND GRADE? IF SO, KEEP READING. OTHERWISE, JUMP TO THE "BULLYING BASICS" SECTION ON PAGE 19.

K-2

HI! MAX AND ZOEY AGAIN.

YOU'VE PROBABLY HEARD THE WORD "BULLYING." BUT WHAT EXACTLY IS IT?

IT IS ALSO WHEN ONE PERSON TURNS FRIENDS AGAINST ANOTHER PERSON.

BULLYING IS WHEN SOMEONE IS MEAN TO ANOTHER PERSON AGAIN AND AGAIN.

SOME PEOPLE BULLY JUST BECAUSE THEY CAN; IT MAKES THEM FEEL GOOD. OTHERS DO IT BECAUSE THEY ARE MAD AT THE PERSON THEY ARE BULLYING.

"BULLYING" IS NOT THE SAME AS "BOTHERING," WHEN SOMEONE IS BEING ANNOYING.

WHEN SOMEONE IS BEING ANNOYING, YOU CAN SIMPLY ASK THAT PERSON TO STOP.

BUT BULLYING IS WHEN SOMEONE BEING MEAN TO YOU MAKES YOU FEEL SAD, SCARED, OR LIKE THERE IS SOMETHING WRONG WITH YOU.

BULLYING IS ALSO WHEN YOU FEEL LOST AND ALONE BECAUSE SOMEONE MADE YOUR FRIENDS STOP LIKING YOU.

BUT WE HAVE GOOD NEWS!

BULLYING IS NOT VERY COMMON IN KINDERGARTEN, FIRST, OR SECOND GRADE.

AND HERE'S EVEN BETTER NEWS! IT'S NOT COMMON IN UPPER GRADES EITHER.

IN GENERAL, MOST BOYS AND GIRLS ARE NEVER BULLIED.

SO IT IS NOT SOMETHING YOU SHOULD WORRY ABOUT.

CHANCES ARE, IT WILL NEVER HAPPEN TO YOU!

HOWEVER, THERE ARE A FEW THINGS YOU CAN DO TO BOTH HELP YOUR FRIENDSHIPS...

...AND MAKE SURE YOU AREN'T BULLIED. BOTH OF THESE ARE EASY TO DO.

4

Learn to Apologize

LOOK AT HOW EASY THIS IS!

I'M SORRY FOR LAUGHING AT YOU.

I KNOW YOU ARE MAD. I WOULD BE TOO.

I PROMISE NOT TO LAUGH AT YOU AGAIN.

NOW, WHAT IF SOMEONE IS MAD...

...BUT YOU DIDN'T DO ANYTHING WRONG?

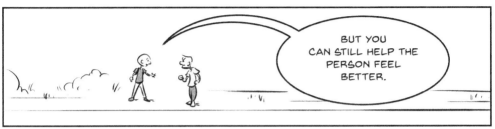

7

REVIEW THE FOUR PARTS OF A GOOD APOLOGY:

1. SAY YOU ARE SORRY.

THIS LETS THE PERSON KNOW THAT YOU FEEL BADLY FOR WHAT YOU DID.

2. SAY WHAT YOU ARE SORRY FOR.

THIS LETS THE PERSON KNOW THAT YOU ACCEPT WHAT YOU DID AND THAT YOU BOTH AGREE ON WHAT YOU DID WRONG.

3. LET THE PERSON KNOW THAT HE OR SHE HAS A RIGHT TO BE MAD.

THIS LETS THE PERSON KNOW THAT IT'S OK TO GET MAD.

4. SAY YOU WILL NOT DO WHATEVER IT WAS YOU DID AGAIN.

THIS LETS THE PERSON KNOW THAT YOU REALLY MEAN IT.

ACTIVITY: PRACTICE!

YES, YOU CAN PRACTICE APOLOGIZING THE RIGHT WAY WITH A FRIEND. THINK OF SOMETHING THAT WOULD MAKE YOUR FRIEND ANGRY, LIKE TAKING A TOY OR BOOK FROM YOUR FRIEND WITHOUT ASKING. THEN SAY THE FOUR-PART APOLOGY. AFTER YOU HAVE PRACTICED APOLOGIZING, HAVE YOUR FRIEND PRACTICE APOLOGIZING TO YOU.

Create a Circle of Friends

GIRLS, THIS SECTION IS FOR YOU. I'M GOING TO TELL YOU ABOUT HAVING A CIRCLE OF FRIENDS.

I KNOW IT'S GREAT TO HAVE A BEST FRIEND. YOU DO EVERYTHING TOGETHER AND TELL EACH OTHER SECRETS.

YOU THINK THAT ONE SPECIAL FRIEND IS ALL YOU NEED.

BUT THE TRUTH IS, FRIENDSHIPS CHANGE.

SOMETIMES OUR BEST FRIEND WANTS A NEW BEST FRIEND. AND THAT CAN REALLY HURT.

IT CAN LEAVE YOU FEELING LOST AND ALONE.

BUT THERE IS SOMETHING YOU CAN DO SO YOU ALWAYS HAVE A FRIEND.

YOU CAN CREATE A CIRCLE OF FRIENDS.

YOU CAN STILL HAVE ONE BEST FRIEND BUT YOU CAN ALSO MAKE MORE FRIENDS.

YOU CAN SIT AS A GROUP AT LUNCH.

YOU CAN PLAY TOGETHER ON THE PLAYGROUND.

YOU CAN HAVE PLAY DATES AS A GROUP.

THIS WAY, IF ONE OF YOUR CIRCLE DECIDES TO MAKE OTHER FRIENDS, YOU WON'T FEEL LOST AND ALONE.

The Strange Trouble with Three

NOW HERE IS SOMETHING YOU MAY HAVE ALREADY EXPERIENCED.

WE CALL IT THE "STRANGE TROUBLE WITH THREE."

DID YOU EVER NOTICE HOW WHEN YOU PLAY WITH ONE OTHER PERSON, IT CAN BE SO MUCH FUN...

...BUT WHEN ANOTHER PERSON JOINS YOU TO MAKE THREE, SOMETIMES ONE PERSON IS LEFT OUT?

THIS IS THE STRANGE TROUBLE WITH THREE. SOMETIMES WHEN THERE ARE THREE, ONE PERSON WILL BE LEFT OUT.

AND EVEN WORSE, SOMETIMES TWO OF THE FRIENDS WILL START BEING MEAN TO THE THIRD FRIEND.

IF YOU ARE WITH TWO OTHER PEOPLE AND THEY AREN'T NICE TO YOU, THIS DOESN'T MEAN THAT THEY DON'T LIKE YOU OR YOU DID ANYTHING WRONG.

IT'S JUST THAT SOMETIMES TWO PEOPLE FEEL LIKE THEY BECOME BETTER FRIENDS IF THEY LEAVE OUT OR ARE MEAN TO A THIRD PERSON.

THAT'S THE STRANGE TROUBLE WITH THREE.

IF YOU ARE PLAYING WITH TWO OTHERS AND THEY START BEING MEAN TO YOU, DO SOMETHING ELSE OR PLAY WITH ANOTHER FRIEND.

AND IF YOU AND A FRIEND ARE LEAVING OUT OR BEING MEAN TO A THIRD FRIEND, REMEMBER THAT FRIENDS SHOULD BE NICE TO EACH OTHER. NO ONE LIKES TO BE LEFT OUT.

AND WHILE SOME GAMES, LIKE CHECKERS, CAN ONLY BE PLAYED BY TWO PEOPLE...

...ALMOST ALL OTHER GAMES CAN BE PLAYED— AND ARE MUCH MORE FUN— WITH THREE!

12

Everyone Is Different

EACH ONE OF US HAS SOMETHING THAT MAKES US DIFFERENT OR UNIQUE.

THAT DIFFERENCE CAN BE A PART OF A PERSON'S APPEARANCE SUCH AS FRIZZY HAIR, A BIG NOSE, A CROOKED SMILE, OR A LARGE TUMMY...

...A MEDICAL CONDITION SUCH AS BEING UNABLE TO WALK, SEE, OR HEAR, OR IF SOMEONE NEEDS MORE TIME TO THINK THINGS THROUGH...

...OR A PERSON'S RACE, CULTURE, OR ETHNICITY THAT MIGHT MAKE THAT PERSON'S SKIN COLOR, HAIR, OR CLOTHING NOT THE SAME AS OUR OWN.

THESE DIFFERENCES MAY BE SIMPLY BECAUSE OF HOW THE PERSON WAS BORN, MAY BE FROM SOMETHING THAT HAPPENED TO THE PERSON, OR MAY BE DUE TO DECISIONS THAT ADULTS MADE FOR THE PERSON.

BEFORE YOU MAKE A REMARK, TEASE, OR JOKE ABOUT SOMEONE ELSE'S DIFFERENCE, REMEMBER THAT WE ARE ALL DIFFERENT IN SOME WAY, AND THAT DIFFERENCE IS JUST WHO WE ARE.

REMARKS ABOUT A PERSON'S DIFFERENCE CAN BE HURTFUL.

SO INSTEAD OF SAYING SOMETHING ABOUT WHAT MAKES THE PERSON DIFFERENT, THINK ABOUT WHAT MAKES THE PERSON JUST LIKE YOU, AND TALK ABOUT THAT!

If Name-calling Makes You Upset

SO IF YOU AREN'T WHAT THE PERSON SAYS YOU ARE, AND YOU KNOW THAT PERSON ISN'T TELLING THE TRUTH, THEN WHY GET UPSET?

BABY!

SOMETIMES PEOPLE CALL OTHERS NAMES JUST TO MAKE THEM UPSET. IF A PERSON DOES NOT GET UPSET, THE PERSON DOING THE NAME-CALLING WILL STOP.

BABY!

GOO, GOO, GAGA!

AND THE BEST WAY TO SHOW YOU ARE NOT UPSET IS TO LAUGH, OR EVEN TURN THE NAME INTO A GAME OR A POEM.

IF SOMEONE IS BOTHERING YOU, FOR EXAMPLE BY CALLING YOU A NAME, REALIZE THAT THE PERSON MAY BE DOING IT JUST TO MAKE YOU UPSET, AND IF YOU DON'T GET UPSET, THE PERSON WILL STOP.

16

If You Are Being Bullied

IF YOU THINK YOU ARE BEING BULLIED—IF SOMEONE IS BEING MEAN TO YOU OVER AND OVER AGAIN—THERE ARE TWO THINGS YOU CAN DO.

FIRST, ASK THE PERSON BEING MEAN TO YOU IF HE OR SHE IS MAD AT YOU FOR SOMETHING.

SOMETIMES WE HURT PEOPLE'S FEELINGS WITHOUT KNOWING IT AND THEY GET MAD.

SO FIND OUT IF THE PERSON IS MAD AND, IF SO, WHY. THEN YOU CAN APOLOGIZE, OR AT LEAST HELP THE PERSON FEEL BETTER.

THE SECOND THING YOU CAN DO IS TO ASK AN ADULT FOR HELP.

A TEACHER OR PARENT CAN BE VERY HELPFUL IN GETTING A PERSON TO STOP BEING MEAN.

REMEMBER, YOU MAY NEVER BE BULLIED, SO IT ISN'T SOMETHING YOU SHOULD WORRY ABOUT.

BUT IT'S GOOD TO APOLOGIZE WHEN YOU'VE HURT SOMEONE'S FEELINGS AND TO HAVE MORE THAN ONE FRIEND.

GOOD LUCK!

BULLYING BASICS

LET'S TALK ABOUT THE BASICS OF BULLYING. WHAT EXACTLY IS BULLYING?

WE ALL KNOW WHAT PEOPLE DO TO BULLY ANOTHER PERSON. THEY...

CALL NAMES

MOCK

MAKE MEAN REMARKS ABOUT APPEARANCE

MAKE MEAN REMARKS ABOUT SKIN COLOR

MAKE MEAN REMARKS ABOUT RELIGION

INTIMIDATE

GLARE

PUSH/SHOVE

EXCLUDE

WHISPER

SPREAD RUMORS

20

SO THE EXACT SAME BEHAVIOR CAN AFFECT PEOPLE DIFFERENTLY. BULLYING BEHAVIOR BETWEEN FRIENDS MAY HAVE NO EFFECT.

THIS IS NOT BULLYING.

OTHERS ARE BOTHERED OR ANNOYED BY THE SAME BEHAVIOR.

THIS IS ALSO NOT BULLYING.

BUT WHEN BULLYING BEHAVIORS MAKE A PERSON FEEL SAD, LOST, ALONE, FRIGHTENED, ANXIOUS, BAD ABOUT HIMSELF OR HERSELF, FLAWED, OR LIKE HE OR SHE DOESN'T BELONG, THAT'S BULLYING.

A SINGLE INSTANCE OF BULLYING BEHAVIOR IS NOT BULLYING; TRUE BULLYING IS WHEN ONE PERSON MAKES ANOTHER PERSON FEEL BAD MORE THAN ONE TIME, USUALLY OVER AND OVER AGAIN.

REMEMBER, "BULLYING" IS NOT THE SAME AS "BOTHERING." IF YOU ARE BEING BOTHERED, ASK THE PERSON TO STOP, OR ASK AN ADULT TO GET THE PERSON TO STOP.

Important Definitions

DON'T WORRY, THERE WON'T BE A QUIZ! BUT THESE WORDS WILL BE USED THROUGHOUT THE GUIDE, SO IT HELPS TO KNOW THEM.

WE DON'T CALL THE PERSON A "BULLY" SINCE THAT TERM IS A LABEL AND DOES NOT FULLY DESCRIBE THE PERSON.

AGGRESSOR:
Person who does the bullying.

"AGGRESSOR" IS USED BECAUSE THE PERSON DOING THE BULLYING IS USING "AGGRESSIVE" BEHAVIOR. AND BECAUSE ANYONE CAN USE AGGRESSIVE BEHAVIOR, ANYONE CAN BE AN *AGGRESSOR*.

A *TARGET* IS THE PERSON WHO IS HARMED BY THE BULLYING BEHAVIOR.

TARGET:
Person who is being bullied.

ANYONE CAN BE A *TARGET* OF BULLYING BEHAVIOR, SO A MORE ACCURATE TERM FOR A PERSON HARMED BY BULLYING IS "AFFECTED TARGET." BUT TO KEEP THINGS SIMPLE, FOR THE REST OF THE GUIDE, WE'LL SIMPLY CALL A PERSON HARMED BY BULLYING A "TARGET."

22

THERE ARE ACTUALLY TWO KINDS OF BULLYING, BOTH OF WHICH HAVE BIG NAMES: "DOMINANCE AGGRESSION" AND "RELATIONAL AGGRESSION."

WE KNOW THESE ARE BIG WORDS, BUT THE BULLYING TYPES ARE REALLY EASY TO UNDERSTAND.

Dominance aggression — Making a person feel scared, bad about himself or herself, or sad by making fun of some aspect of his or her body, background, or culture; putting him or her down; or by pushing, shoving, or using threatening gestures

THIS TYPE OF BULLYING MAKES AN AGGRESSOR FEEL OR APPEAR STRONGER OR MORE POWERFUL THAN THE TARGET; THE AGGRESSOR IS "DOMINANT." IN OTHER WORDS, THIS IS "BOY BULLYING."

NO, GIRLS DO IT, TOO.

BUT MOSTLY BOYS.

BOTH BOYS AND GIRLS BULLY IN THIS WAY.

Relational Aggression – Making a person feel lost, alone, bad about herself or himself, or sad by hurting the person's friendships with others by doing things such as gossiping, starting a rumor, betraying the person, starting a secret petition about the person, and excluding the person from groups

THIS TYPE OF BULLYING IS COMMONLY THOUGHT OF AS "GIRL BULLYING."

TRUE.

GLAD YOU AGREE. WHILE BOTH GIRLS AND BOYS CAN USE RELATIONAL AGGRESSION, IT IS MOST COMMON AMONG GIRLS.

24

Why Do People Bully?

PEOPLE BULLY FOR A NUMBER OF REASONS:

To RETALIATE
for an actual or perceived offense

TO GET A FEELING OF
POWER
OVER ANOTHER PERSON

TO EXCLUDE
IN ORDER TO REAFFIRM A GROUP'S MEMBERSHIP OR MAKE SOMEONE FEEL LIKE HE OR SHE NO LONGER BELONGS

As a way for the aggressor to
GET SOME-THING

TO BE MORE POPULAR
OR MAKE NEW FRIENDS

For fun and to
MAKE OTHERS LAUGH,
which gives a feeling of being superior

Because of an **ANGER PROBLEM** or other psychological condition

UNFORTUNATELY, BECAUSE BULLYING IS HUMAN, IT IS HERE TO STAY. ALTHOUGH AGGRESSIVE BEHAVIOR CANNOT BE STOPPED, THERE ARE THINGS YOU CAN DO TO STOP BULLYING. READ ON!

How People Bully and the TOP SECRET FACTS They Don't Want You to Know

KNOWING HOW BULLYING WORKS IS IMPORTANT, AS IT THEN ALLOWS INTENDED TARGETS TO PREVENT IT FROM HAPPENING IN THE FIRST PLACE AND TO STOP IT FROM HAPPENING IF IT IS IN PROGRESS.

THERE ARE THREE KEY WAYS THAT PEOPLE BULLY: PHYSICAL INTIMIDATION, THE USE OF CHARACTERISTICS, AND HARMING FRIENDSHIPS.

PHYSICAL INTIMIDATION

AGGRESSORS SCARE TARGETS BY MAKING THEM THINK THEY WILL BE PHYSICALLY HARMED.

THE AGGRESSOR CAN MAKE THREATS...

...STAND IN AN INTIMIDATING WAY...

...GIVE MEAN LOOKS..

...AND PUSH AND SHOVE THE TARGET.

THIS IS TYPICAL OF "BOY BULLYING."

YOU MEAN "DOMINANCE AGGRESSION."

BUT HERE'S THE SECRET:

28

GIRLS KNOW THAT WHAT IS MOST IMPORTANT TO OTHER GIRLS ARE FRIENDSHIPS.

SO THE BEST WAY TO HURT ANOTHER GIRL IS TO DAMAGE HER FRIENDSHIPS.

THAT IS WHY GIRLS WILL BULLY OTHERS BY TURNING THEIR FRIENDS AGAINST THEM, EMBARRASSING THEM, AND EXCLUDING THEM. BUT HERE'S THE SECRET:

TOP SECRET #3a:

AGGRESSORS MAY START BULLYING DUE TO SOME KIND OF A CONFLICT; THE AGGRESSOR WILL BE ANGRY AT THE TARGET FOR SOMETHING. IF THE CONFLICT IS RESOLVED— IF THE TARGET AND AGGRESSOR TALK ABOUT IT AND, IF NECESSARY, THE TARGET CAN APOLOGIZE— THEN THE BULLYING WILL LIKELY STOP.

HAVE I OFFENDED YOU?

I'M SORRY FOR...

TOP SECRET #3b:

BULLYING ALSO STARTS DUE TO JEALOUSY OVER A SPECIAL FRIEND, A SKILL THE TARGET HAS, OR SOMETHING THE TARGET POSSESSES THAT SETS HER APART FROM OTHERS IN A GOOD WAY.

IF THE TARGET CAN TALK TO THE AGGRESSOR AND THEY GET TO KNOW EACH OTHER BETTER, THIS CAN SOMETIMES STOP THE BULLYING.

NOW THAT YOU KNOW THE BASICS, FIND YOUR SECTION:

Find Your Section

TO HELP SOMEONE WHO IS BEING BULLIED, *GO TO PAGE 32.*

TO LEARN WAYS OF INTERACTING WITH AGGRESSORS SO THAT YOU AREN'T BULLIED, *GO TO PAGE 42.*

TO STOP SOMEONE FROM BULLYING YOU, *GO TO PAGE 68.*

AGGRESS DOMINA

TO TEACH A PARENT HOW TO HELP YOU, *GO TO PAGE 76.*

DOING SOMETHING ABOUT BULLYING: BYSTANDER INTERVENTION

LET'S TALK ABOUT WHAT YOU CAN DO TO HELP STOP BULLYING IF YOU SEE IT HAPPENING.

SAY YOU SEE SOMEONE BEING BULLIED.

OR A CLASSMATE SPREADS AN EMBARRASSING RUMOR ABOUT SOMEONE THAT CAN'T POSSIBLY BE TRUE.

YOU WANT TO DO SOMETHING TO STOP THE BULLYING...

...BUT YOU ARE NOT SURE WHAT TO DO.

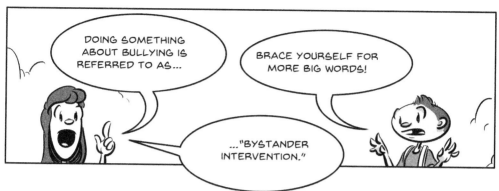

DOING SOMETHING ABOUT BULLYING IS REFERRED TO AS...

BRACE YOURSELF FOR MORE BIG WORDS!

..."BYSTANDER INTERVENTION."

AND WE'LL BE HONEST: DOING SOMETHING ABOUT BULLYING *ISN'T* EASY.

YOU MAY BE AFRAID THE AGGRESSOR WILL START BULLYING *YOU.*

YIKES!

AND DOING SOMETHING CAN FEEL LIKE YOU ARE CHOOSING SIDES AGAINST SOMEONE WHO MAY BE MORE POPULAR THAN THE PERSON YOU ARE TRYING TO HELP.

YOU MAY WORRY THAT YOU ARE RISKING YOUR OWN FRIENDSHIPS JUST TO HELP SOMEONE WHO MAY NOT REALLY BE YOUR FRIEND.

BUT THERE ARE MANY WAYS TO HELP STOP BULLYING WITHOUT FEAR OF BEING BULLIED OR FEELING LIKE YOU HAVE TO CHOOSE SIDES. THESE ACTIONS ARE CALLED "INDIRECT INTERVENTION."

Indirect Intervention

REFUSE TO PARTICIPATE IN THE BULLYING

DON'T LAUGH, MAKE ADDITIONAL COMMENTS, OR EVEN STAND LIKE YOU'RE ON THE SIDE OF THE AGGRESSOR. DON'T JOIN IN.

DON'T REWARD THE AGGRESSOR

DON'T SHOW ADMIRATION FOR AN AGGRESSOR OR APPROVAL OF BULLYING.

IN PRIVATE, SUPPORT THE TARGET

LET THE TARGET KNOW THAT YOU DON'T LIKE THE BULLYING EITHER. YOU CAN ALSO SUGGEST THAT THE TARGET GET HELP.

THAT GUY WAS A REAL JERK.

BE A FRIEND TO THE TARGET

DO YOU WANT TO SIT TOGETHER AT LUNCH?

WHEN SOMEONE FEELS ALONE DUE TO BULLYING, IT HELPS TO HAVE A FRIEND.

SUGGEST THAT THE TARGET TALK TO THE AGGRESSOR

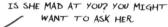

IS SHE MAD AT YOU? YOU MIGHT WANT TO ASK HER.

YOU CAN ASK THE TARGET IF THERE IS A CONFLICT AND ENCOURAGE HER TO APOLOGIZE, OR AT LEAST TALK TO THE AGGRESSOR.

SUGGEST THAT THE AGGRESSOR RESOLVE THE CONFLICT THROUGH TALKING AND NOT BULLYING

IN PRIVATE, ASK THE AGGRESSOR IF HE OR SHE IS MAD. IF SO, SUGGEST HE OR SHE TALK TO THE TARGET TO RESOLVE THE PROBLEM.

HEY, WHAT'D THAT KID DO TO YOU?

THAT "SMART GUY" MOCKED ME IN SCIENCE CLASS.

I KNOW HIM. I'M SURE HE DIDN'T MEAN IT. GO TALK TO HIM.

IN PRIVATE, ASK THE AGGRESSOR TO STOP THE BULLYING

IF YOU KNOW THE AGGRESSOR, YOU CAN TRY ASKING HER TO STOP. SOMETIMES DISAPPROVAL FROM FRIENDS OR CLASSMATES WILL WORK.

STOP BEING MEAN TO HER. IT'S NOT COOL.

What You Can Do About GIRL BULLYING

BE A FRIEND: INCLUDE

DON'T PARTICIPATE

BE A FRIEND: TALK ABOUT IT

NOTIFY TARGET

RELATIONAL AGGRESSION USUALLY REQUIRES THE PARTICIPATION OF OTHER GIRLS. THE EASIEST WAY TO STOP THIS KIND OF BULLYING IS NOT TO PARTICIPATE. AND YOU CAN ENLIST THE HELP OF YOUR FRIENDS; PLEDGE TO TRY TO STOP IT TOGETHER. THERE ARE MANY DIFFERENT PATHS YOU CAN TAKE TO HELP STOP THE BULLYING.

FIND OUT SOURCE

MORE WAYS TO HELP

WHO TOLD YOU THAT?

MARY!

HELP RESOLVE CONFLICT

HEY MARY, DID YOU START A RUMOR?

WHAT OF IT?

DID JILL DO SOMETHING TO YOU?

YES, SHE SAID I WAS FAT.

TALK TO HER ABOUT IT. RUMORS ONLY MAKE THINGS WORSE.

OKAY, YOU'RE RIGHT.

NO.

NOTIFY TARGET

WHAT DO I CARE?

HEY JILL, I THINK MARY IS UPSET WITH YOU. YOU SHOULD TALK TO HER.

What You Can Do About Boy Bullying

IF YOU SEE BOY BULLYING HAPPENING...

HE MEANS "DOMINANCE AGGRESSION."

...YOU CAN TRY TELLING THE AGGRESSOR TO STOP, OR YOU CAN DISRUPT THE BULLYING BY PRETENDING TO BE UNAWARE OR NOT TO CARE. HERE ARE EXAMPLES; YOU CAN SAY WHAT YOU THINK IS BEST.

PRETEND TO BE UNAWARE: DISRUPT THE BULLYING

HEY GUYS, WHAT'S GOING ON?

PRETEND TO BE UNAWARE: DIVERT ATTENTION

DO YOU GUYS WANT TO KICK A BALL AROUND?

BE AWARE BUT DON'T CARE: CHANGE THE CHANNEL

BE DIRECT: STOP THE BULLYING

KEEP IN MIND THAT SOMETIMES IT IS HARD TO TELL THE DIFFERENCE BETWEEN BULLYING AND JUST FOOLING AROUND.

IT CAN BE TOTALLY EMBARRASSING IF YOU STEP IN TO STOP BULLYING AND IT TURNS OUT TO BE JUST FRIENDS PLAYING AROUND.

IF YOU AREN'T SURE, KEEP OBSERVING.

IF YOU SEE IT HAPPENING AGAIN, AND ONE PERSON APPEARS SAD OR UPSET, IT'S PROBABLY BULLYING AND YOU CAN TAKE ACTION.

ONE FINAL BUT *EXTREMELY* IMPORTANT NOTE: SOMETIMES PEOPLE WHO ARE BULLIED ARE SO UPSET THAT THEY WANT TO HURT THEMSELVES TO ESCAPE THEIR PAIN OR GET ATTENTION OR THEY WANT TO HURT OTHERS.

IF YOU BECOME AWARE OF A PERSON WHO TALKS OR WRITES ABOUT TAKING HIS OR HER OWN LIFE OR PERFORMING A VIOLENT ACT AGAINST OTHER STUDENTS OR THE SCHOOL, TELL AT LEAST TWO ADULTS *IMMEDIATELY.*

AND YOU ARE *NOT* BEING A TATTLETALE. IT IS OKAY TO TELL TO KEEP SOMEONE OUT OF TROUBLE. YOUR ACTION COULD SAVE A LIFE.

BULLYPROOF YOURSELF:
How to Keep Others from Bullying You

LET'S TALK ABOUT HOW YOU CAN STOP SOMEONE FROM BULLYING YOU.

BOY BULLYING...

...IS USUALLY DIRECT AND CONFRONTATIONAL. THE AGGRESSOR'S GOAL IS TO MAKE YOU FEEL BAD (SCARED, WORRIED, OR FLAWED).

HE MEANS "DOMINANCE AGGRESSION."

THE BULLYING BEHAVIOR SUCCEEDS WHEN IT MAKES YOU FEEL BAD (AND THE AGGRESSOR CAN SEE IT) AND FAILS WHEN IT DOES NOT. SO HOW YOU REACT TO THE BULLYING DETERMINES WHETHER OR NOT IT SUCCEEDS. IF YOU DON'T FEEL BAD, OR FEEL BAD BUT DON'T SHOW IT, THE AGGRESSOR GETS NO SATISFACTION AND THE BULLYING FAILS.

SUCCEEDS: YOU FEEL SAD, SCARED, OR FLAWED. AGGRESSOR FEELS GOOD.

FAILS: YOU ARE NOT OR DON'T APPEAR AFFECTED. AGGRESSOR GETS NO SATISFACTION.

RELATIONAL AGGRESSION...

ALSO KNOWN AS "GIRL BULLYING."

...IS DIFFERENT. RELATIONAL AGGRESSION IS OFTEN COVERT, SO YOU DON'T KNOW IT IS HAPPENING UNTIL DAMAGE HAS BEEN DONE. BECAUSE OF THAT, THE BEST WAY TO DEAL WITH RELATIONAL AGGRESSION IS TO PREVENT IT FROM HAPPENING IN THE FIRST PLACE. BUT IF IT DOES START, THERE ARE THINGS YOU CAN DO TO STOP IT.

BOY AND GIRL BULLYING SOMETIMES STARTS WHEN ONE PERSON OFFENDS ANOTHER PERSON. THE OFFENDED PERSON MAY TRY TO "GET BACK" AT THE OTHER PERSON. IF SOMEONE KEEPS TRYING TO BULLY YOU, ASK THAT PERSON IF HE OR SHE IS MAD AT YOU. IF SO, YOU CAN FIND OUT WHY AND RESOLVE THE PROBLEM.

GIRLS, THIS IS ESPECIALLY IMPORTANT FOR YOU! IF SOMEONE STARTS TO BULLY YOU, FIND OUT IF YOU'VE OFFENDED THAT PERSON SO YOU CAN APOLOGIZE.

USE THE FOUR-PART APOLOGY

IF SOMEONE IS MAD AT YOU, JUST SAYING "SORRY" MAY NOT BE ENOUGH.

YOU ALSO SHOULD SAY WHAT YOU DID WRONG, AGREE THAT THE OTHER PERSON HAS A RIGHT TO BE MAD, AND PROMISE NOT TO DO IT AGAIN.

SQUEAK SQUEAK SQUEAK

THIS IS THE FORMULA:

FOR EXAMPLE, SAY, "I'M SORRY FOR LAUGHING AT YOU. YOU HAVE EVERY RIGHT TO BE MAD. I PROMISE NOT TO DO IT AGAIN." IT'S THAT EASY!

Say sorry + SPECIFY OFFENDING ACTION + ACKNOWLEDGE ANGER + PROMISE NOT TO DO IT AGAIN.

PEOPLE FACE DOMINANCE AGGRESSION DAILY. HOWEVER, SOME PEOPLE ARE NOT AFFECTED BY IT. WHY?

BECAUSE SOME PEOPLE EITHER HAVE LEARNED OR ALREADY KNOW HOW TO REACT OR RESPOND TO BULLYING IN A WAY THAT MAKES IT FAIL.

HERE ARE EXAMPLES OF WAYS OF REACTING TO DOMINANCE AGGRESSION THAT ALLOWS IT TO SUCCEED, AND WAYS TO MAKE IT FAIL.

INTIMIDATION

SUCCEEDS: COWER, SHRINK BACK, SHOW FEAR, OR TRY TO GET AWAY.

FAILS: SHOW NO FEAR. STAND TALL AND HOLD YOUR GROUND, PRETEND NOT TO BE AFRAID, WALK WITH CONFIDENCE, AND LOOK THE AGGRESSOR IN THE EYE.

REMEMBER, AGGRESSORS RARELY INTEND PHYSICAL HARM. THEY JUST WANT TO **SCARE** YOU.

MEAN REMARK

SUCCEEDS: GET MAD, SAD, FRUSTRATED, OR MAKE A MEAN REMARK BACK.

FAILS: PRETEND NOT TO BE BOTHERED OR DO SOMETHING UNEXPECTED, LIKE LAUGH AT THE REMARK (NOT AT THE AGGRESSOR!) OR AGREE WITH THE AGGRESSOR.

PLEASE NOTE THAT PRETENDING NOT TO BE BOTHERED IS **NOT** THE SAME THING AS IGNORING THE REMARK. LET THE AGGRESSOR KNOW YOU HEARD IT SO THAT YOU CAN SHOW YOU AREN'T BOTHERED.

DEMANDS FOR ITEMS OR MONEY

SUCCEEDS: SHOW FEAR AND HAND OVER THE ITEMS OR MONEY.

FAILS: SAY "NO" LIKE A FRIEND. SAY, "I WISH I COULD BUT..." OR "I'D LOVE TO BUT..." AND GIVE A REASON WHY YOU CAN'T.

IF YOU SAY THAT YOU WOULD LOVE TO HELP THE AGGRESSOR AS THOUGH YOU ARE A GOOD FRIEND, IT MAKES IT **HARDER** FOR THE AGGRESSOR TO TRY TO BULLY YOU.

LIGHT PHYSICAL CONTACT SUCH AS SHOVING

SUCCEEDS: SHOW FEAR OR GET UPSET.

FAILS: SHOW NO FEAR, DON'T GET UPSET, OR CALMLY SAY IT ISN'T COOL.

REALLY HURTING SOMEONE ISN'T BULLYING. DEFEND YOURSELF BUT **DON'T** FIGHT BACK. GET AWAY AND **IMMEDIATELY** TELL AN ADULT.

SUCCEEDS: FEEL FLAWED OR LIKE YOU NEED TO CHANGE.

FAILS: SHOW PRIDE IN WHO YOU ARE, HOW YOU DRESS, AND HOW YOU LOOK.

DON'T FORGET, EVERYONE IS **UNIQUE** AND DIFFERENT IN SOME WAY.

REMEMBER, THE AGGRESSOR WANTS TO FEEL LIKE HE OR SHE HAS POWER OVER YOU AND CAN MAKE YOU AFRAID OR UPSET.

IF YOU SHOW NO FEAR OR DON'T GET UPSET, YOU TAKE AWAY THAT FEELING OF POWER AND THE **BULLYING** FAILS.

AND YOU CAN'T SIMPLY IGNORE BULLYING BEHAVIOR; AN AGGRESSOR WILL KNOW HE OR SHE IS UPSETTING YOU IF YOU JUST TRY TO PRETEND IT ISN'T HAPPENING AND HOPE IT WILL STOP. YOU HAVE TO ACTIVELY RESPOND TO THE BULLYING IN SOME WAY TO SHOW THAT YOU ARE **NOT** AFFECTED.

ALSO, THESE WAYS OF REACTING TO BULLYING TO GET IT TO STOP CAN TAKE TIME BECAUSE YOU AREN'T SIMPLY ACTING DIFFERENTLY — YOU HAVE TO CONVINCE THE AGGRESSOR THAT YOU ARE NO LONGER AFFECTED. IF IT DOESN'T WORK THE FIRST TIME, **KEEP TRYING!**

GIRLS, THIS SECTION IS FOR YOU. I'M GOING TO TELL YOU ABOUT WAYS YOU CAN PREVENT RELATIONAL AGGRESSION FROM STARTING, HOW TO STOP IT WHEN IT DOES, AND METHODS TO DEAL WITH IT IF IT SUCCEEDS.

GIRLS, I KNOW I'M GENERALIZING, BUT WE USUALLY DON'T TELL OUR FRIENDS WHEN OR WHY WE ARE ANGRY, AND WE VALUE OUR FRIENDS ABOVE **ALL** ELSE (WHICH IS WHY WE KEEP OUR ANGER TO OURSELVES). WE OFTEN USE RELATIONAL AGGRESSION INSTEAD OF TELLING SOMEONE THAT WE ARE ANGRY. RELATIONAL AGGRESSION AVOIDS CONFRONTATION, AND WE THINK IT WILL ALLOW US TO PRESERVE THE FRIENDSHIP WHILE GETTING JUSTICE FOR THE OFFENSE.

BUT RELATIONAL AGGRESSION DOESN'T RESOLVE THE CONFLICT; WE CAN HURT OUR FRIENDS MORE THAN WE INTEND, AND FRIENDS CAN DO THE SAME TO US, CREATING A HUGE MESS. **EXPRESSING** ANGER, **OWNING UP** TO OUR ACTIONS, AND **APOLOGIZING** THE RIGHT WAY ARE THE KEYS TO PREVENTING AND STOPPING RELATIONAL AGGRESSION.

OF COURSE, SOME RELATIONAL AGGRESSION DOES NOT **START** FROM CONFLICT; IT CAN ARISE FROM JEALOUSY, FROM WANTING TO BE MORE POPULAR, TO STRENGTHEN FRIENDSHIPS IN A GROUP BY TARGETING AN OUTSIDER, AND SIMPLY BECAUSE SOME GIRLS FEEL GOOD WHEN DOING IT. IN THESE CASES, TALKING TO AGGRESSORS **DIRECTLY** SO THEY GET TO KNOW YOU AND HAVING A LARGE CIRCLE OF FRIENDS WHO CAN STAND BY YOU CAN HELP.

AVOID USING RELATIONAL AGGRESSION

WE DON'T WANT RELATIONAL AGGRESSION DIRECTED AT **US**, SO WE NEED TO LEARN NOT TO USE IT AGAINST **OTHERS**. IF A GIRL MAKES YOU ANGRY...

...INSTEAD OF GIVING HER THE SILENT TREATMENT OR USING RELATIONAL AGGRESSION TO GET BACK AT HER, JUST TELL HER THAT YOU ARE ANGRY AND WHY AND RESOLVE IT.

SO YOU CAN EITHER DO THIS:

SUPPRESS

SILENT TREATMENT

RELATIONAL AGGRESSION

OR DO THIS:

EXPRESS YOUR ANGER

LISTEN TO APOLOGY

ACCEPT APOLOGY

RESOLVE AND MOVE ON

IF YOU TALK ABOUT IT AND RESOLVE IT, YOU'LL BE BETTER FRIENDS THAN EVER.

ANOTHER REASON WE USE RELATIONAL AGGRESSION IS TO AVOID TELLING A FRIEND THAT WE DON'T WANT TO BE FRIENDS ANYMORE.

AS HARD AS IT IS, TELL HER DIRECTLY THAT YOU WANT TO HANG OUT WITH OTHER FRIENDS.

ways to prevent relational aggression

THE BEST WAY TO STOP RELATIONAL AGGRESSION IS TO PREVENT IT FROM STARTING IN THE FIRST PLACE. TARGETS ARE OFTEN UNAWARE OF WHEN IT STARTS, AND RELATIONAL AGGRESSION CAN BE HARD TO STOP. THE FOLLOWING ACTIONS CAN HELP PREVENT RELATIONAL AGGRESSION FROM STARTING.

LISTEN WHEN SOMEONE IS ANGRY WITH YOU, OWN UP TO YOUR ACTIONS, AND USE THE FOUR-PART APOLOGY.

YOU'VE SAID SOMETHING MEAN ABOUT YOUR FRIEND TO ANOTHER GIRL.

YOUR FRIEND FINDS OUT AND IS ANGRY.

SHE FINDS THE COURAGE TO TELL YOU DIRECTLY.

52

ACCEPT AN APOLOGY AND MOVE ON.

YOUR FRIEND SAID SOMETHING EMBARRASSING ABOUT YOU TO YOUR OTHER FRIENDS. SHE REALIZES THAT SHE HURT YOU AND SHE'S SORRY. SHE APOLOGIZES.

I'M SORRY FOR...

DEVELOP A FRIENDSHIP CIRCLE

YOU HAVE ONE GOOD FRIEND-YOUR BEST FRIEND-AND YOU DON'T FEEL LIKE YOU NEED ANY OTHER FRIENDS. BUT YOU KNOW THAT SOMETIMES FRIENDSHIPS CHANGE, AND YOU DON'T WANT TO BE WITHOUT FRIENDS.

OPTION 1: CHANCE IT

HI!

YOU DECIDE TO TAKE THE CHANCE AND ONLY HAVE YOUR BEST FRIEND. BUT THIS CAN MEAN DISASTER IF SHE WANTS TO HAVE NEW FRIENDS OR SOMEONE TURNS HER AGAINST YOU.

OPTION 2: MAKE MORE FRIENDS

YOU REALIZE YOU CAN KEEP YOUR BEST FRIEND AND HAVE MORE FRIENDS. SO EVEN IF YOUR BEST FRIEND MAKES NEW FRIENDS OR SOMEONE TRIES TO BULLY YOU, YOU'LL STILL HAVE LOTS OF FRIENDS AND YOU WILL BE OKAY.

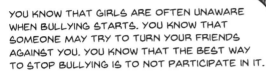

MAKE A FRIENDSHIP PACT

YOU KNOW THAT GIRLS ARE OFTEN UNAWARE WHEN BULLYING STARTS. YOU KNOW THAT SOMEONE MAY TRY TO TURN YOUR FRIENDS AGAINST YOU. YOU KNOW THAT THE BEST WAY TO STOP BULLYING IS TO NOT PARTICIPATE IN IT.

WE'RE ALL GOOD FRIENDS...

...BUT SHOULD WE MAKE A PACT?

OPTION 1: DO NOTHING

YOU CAN DO NOTHING AND HOPE THAT BULLYING NEVER HAPPENS TO YOU.

OPTION 2: MAKE A PACT

YOU CAN GET YOUR FRIENDS TOGETHER AND MAKE A FRIENDSHIP PACT, AN AGREEMENT TO NEVER PARTICIPATE IN BULLYING AGAINST EACH OTHER.

NEVER PAY A PRICE FOR FRIENDSHIP

A POPULAR GIRL APPROACHES YOU AT THE MALL AND SUGGESTS YOU HANG OUT WITH HER. YOU ARE FLATTERED, AS YOU'VE ALWAYS WANTED TO BE HER FRIEND. BUT FIRST, SHE WANTS YOU TO STEAL SOMETHING FROM A STORE FOR HER TO "PROVE" YOU CAN BE A GOOD FRIEND.

OPTION 1: BUSTED!

YOU'RE CAUGHT! AND LOOK WHERE YOUR "FRIEND" IS NOW.

OPTION 2: SUCKER!

YOU STEAL THE ITEM AND GIVE IT TO HER, AND SHE'S SUDDENLY NO LONGER INTERESTED IN BEING FRIENDS.

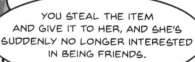

OPTION 3: REFUSE TO BE USED

YOU REFUSE; YOU KNOW THAT SHE DOESN'T REALLY WANT TO BE YOUR FRIEND BUT IS USING YOU. YOU KNOW THAT TRUE FRIENDSHIP CANNOT BE BOUGHT.

NEVER POST ONLINE, EMAIL, OR TEXT WHEN ANGRY

YOU GET AN EMAIL WITH A MEAN REMARK ABOUT YOUR HAIR FROM ONE OF YOUR FRIENDS. SHE HAS COPIED WHAT SEEMS LIKE HALF THE CLASS. YOU ARE FURIOUS.

OPTION 1: REACT

YOU "REPLY ALL" WITH A MEAN COMMENT ABOUT YOUR FRIEND. NOW YOU ARE BOTH ANGRY. FRIENDS START TO TAKE SIDES. A "WAR" HAS BEGUN.

OPTION 2: TALK DIRECTLY

YOU WAIT UNTIL YOU FEEL CALM AND THEN TALK DIRECTLY TO YOUR FRIEND. SHE APOLOGIZES AND EVEN AGREES TO SEND ANOTHER EMAIL TO EVERY-ONE WITH HER APOLOGY. YOU ACCEPT THE APOLOGY AND MOVE ON.

DON'T TAKE EMBARRASSING PICTURES OR VIDEOS YOU WOULDN'T WANT THE WORLD TO SEE.

YOUR BEST FRIEND FOUND A FUNNY OUTFIT IN AN OLD TRUNK IN HER ATTIC. SHE SUGGESTS TAKING A PHOTO OF YOU IN THE FUNNY OUTFIT.

OPTION 1: AGREE

YOU LET HER TAKE YOUR PICTURE. TWO DAYS LATER, SHE GETS ANGRY WITH YOU BUT INSTEAD OF TELLING YOU DIRECTLY, SHE EMAILS THE PHOTO TO ALL OF YOUR FRIENDS.

OPTION 2: REFUSE

YOU KNOW THAT THE PICTURE COULD ONE DAY APPEAR ONLINE. YOU POLITELY REFUSE AND SUGGEST YOU DO SOMETHING ELSE.

Counteracting Relational Aggression

SOMETIMES, DESPITE EVERYTHING YOU DO TO PREVENT RELATIONAL AGGRESSION, IT HAPPENS. HERE ARE SOME THINGS YOU CAN DO IF YOU ARE THE TARGET OF RELATIONAL AGGRESSION.

IF SOMETHING FEELS WRONG, INVESTIGATE

YOU WAKE UP ONE MORNING. YOUR WORLD FEELS TURNED UPSIDE DOWN. FRIENDS ARE SUDDENLY AVOIDING YOU OR ACTING STRANGE.

YAWN

NO MESSAGES

IDENTIFY AND TALK TO THE AGGRESSOR

SOMEONE IS BULLYING YOU. IF YOU DON'T FIND OUT WHO IT IS, IT MAY CONTINUE AND RUIN YOUR FRIENDSHIPS. YOU NEED TO FIND OUT WHO STARTED THE AGGRESSION.

WHO STARTED THIS?

IT WAS BECKY.

OPTION 1: AVOID AGGRESSOR

IF YOU DON'T TALK TO THE AGGRESSOR, THE DAMAGE TO YOUR FRIENDSHIPS MAY TAKE A LONG TIME TO FIX.

OPTION 2: TALK TO AGGRESSOR

TALK TO THE AGGRESSOR. APOLOGIZE IF YOU'VE OFFENDED HER, AND ASK HER TO STOP AND HELP REPAIR THE DAMAGE.

WHY DID YOU DO IT? HAVE I OFFENDED YOU?

YOU HAVE A FRIEND WHO IS NICE TO YOU – MOST OF THE TIME. BUT SHE ALSO SAYS AND DOES MEAN THINGS TO YOU WHEN YOU ARE ALONE AND AROUND OTHERS. SOMETIMES WHEN YOU ARE WITH HER YOU FEEL GREAT ABOUT YOURSELF, BUT SOMETIMES YOUR FRIEND MAKES YOU FEEL BAD ABOUT YOURSELF.

OPTION 1: STAY

YOU CAN KEEP THIS FRIEND, KNOWING THAT YOU'LL FEEL GOOD ON SOME DAYS AND BAD ON OTHERS. BUT A FRIENDSHIP THAT IS NOT REAL WILL NEVER FEEL RIGHT AND CAN MAKE YOU DOUBT YOURSELF.

OPTION 2: GO

YOU RECOGNIZE THAT SINCE SHE DOES MEAN THINGS, SHE ISN'T A REAL FRIEND. YOU TELL HER THAT YOU NO LONGER WANT TO BE FRIENDS. WHEN YOU GIVE UP A FRIENDSHIP THAT IS NOT REAL, YOU CAN REGAIN YOUR CONFIDENCE AND HAVE THE OPPORTUNITY TO MAKE A REAL FRIEND.

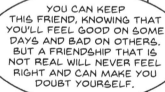

DON'T ACCEPT THE SILENT TREATMENT; FIGURE OUT AND RESOLVE THE PROBLEM.

IF A FRIEND IS NOT TALKING TO YOU, DON'T JUST ASSUME IT IS YOUR FAULT AND WAIT FOR THE SILENT TREATMENT TO PASS. FIND OUT WHY SHE IS UPSET AND, IF NECESSARY, APOLOGIZE.

OPTION 1: LET IT GO

I'M STILL MAD

IF YOU DON'T ADDRESS THE PROBLEM, YOUR FRIEND WILL STILL BE ANGRY EVEN IF SHE DOESN'T SHOW IT. THE ANGER WILL ERUPT LATER, OR SHE MAY TRY TO GET BACK AT YOU THROUGH RELATIONAL AGGRESSION.

OPTION 2: DON'T LET IT GO

PLEASE TELL ME WHY YOU ARE MAD.

FINE. YOU DID...

IF YOU FIND OUT WHY SHE IS MAD, YOU CAN APOLOGIZE, SHE CAN FORGIVE YOU, AND YOU BOTH CAN BE FRIENDS AGAIN.

IF YOU ARE SUFFERING THE LOSS OF FRIENDS AND FEELING ALONE BECAUSE OF BULLYING, KNOW THAT, AS BAD AS YOU MAY FEEL NOW, THINGS WILL GET BETTER IN TIME.

AS MUCH AS IT HURTS, SOMETIMES FRIENDSHIPS CANNOT BE REPAIRED, OR THE REPAIR CAN TAKE A LONG TIME.

BUT THINGS WILL GET BETTER, *I PROMISE!*

GETTING BULLYING TO STOP!

YOU'RE BEING BULLIED. IT'S HARD TO ADMIT, EVEN TO YOURSELF. YOU MAY FEEL LIKE THERE IS SOMETHING WRONG WITH YOU OR THAT THE BULLYING IS YOUR FAULT. YOU MAY FEEL LIKE YOU ARE WEAK OR UNPOPULAR. YOU MAY HAVE LOST YOUR FRIENDS, OR FRIENDS MAY NOW BE EXCLUDING YOU, AND YOU HAVE NO IDEA WHY. YOU MAY FEEL LOST, ALONE, OR SCARED. WHAT SHOULD YOU DO?

FIRST, YOU NEED TO REALIZE THAT **THE BULLYING IS NOT YOUR FAULT.** NO MATTER WHO YOU ARE, WHERE YOU ARE FROM, WHAT YOU LOOK LIKE, OR WHAT YOU BELIEVE IN, NO ONE DESERVES TO BE BULLIED. YOU ARE BEING BULLIED BECAUSE SOMEONE OR A GROUP OF PEOPLE ARE BEING MEAN TO YOU.

SECOND, YOU NEED TO BELIEVE THAT **YOU ARE NOT FLAWED.** IF YOUR AGGRESSOR MAKES FUN OF SOME PART OF YOU--FOR EXAMPLE, A PART OF YOUR BODY, YOUR ETHNICITY, OR YOUR RELIGION--THAT DOES NOT MEAN ANYTHING IS WRONG WITH YOU. EVERYBODY IS UNIQUE IN SOME WAY, EVEN AGGRESSORS! BUT AGGRESSORS WILL USE ANYTHING AS AN EXCUSE TO BULLY. SO YOU MUST UNDERSTAND AND BELIEVE THAT YOU AREN'T FLAWED; THE AGGRESSOR JUST WANTS TO HAVE AN EXCUSE FOR BEING MEAN.

FOURTH, YOU NEED TO **DECIDE IF YOU WANT AN ADULT HELPER.** YES, WE KNOW—AN ADULT MAY BE THE LAST PERSON YOU MAY WANT TO TALK TO. NOT ONLY IS IT HARD TO ADMIT TO BEING BULLIED, BUT YOU'RE ALSO WORRIED THE ADULT MIGHT MAKE THINGS WORSE. YOU CERTAINLY DON'T WANT THE AGGRESSOR TO KNOW YOU'VE TOLD OR TO GET IN TROUBLE AND THEN TAKE IT OUT ON YOU. AND MOST IMPORTANTLY, YOU WANT TO SOLVE THIS PROBLEM YOURSELF.

BUT WOULDN'T IT BE GOOD TO HAVE SOMEONE TO TALK TO WHEN YOU ARE FEELING SCARED AND ALONE? WOULDN'T IT BE GREAT TO TALK ABOUT THE INTERACTION SKILLS YOU ARE TRYING OUT AND REPORT BACK ON HOW THEY ARE WORKING? WOULDN'T IT BE HELPFUL TO TALK TO SOMEONE WHO HAS ALREADY FACED AND GONE THROUGH THE SAME THINGS THAT YOU ARE FACING NOW?

GETTING ADULT HELP DOES **NOT** MEAN THE ADULT IS GOING TO TALK TO THE AGGRESSOR, GET THE AGGRESSOR IN TROUBLE, OR MAKE THINGS WORSE. THE FACT IS, ADULTS CAN BE A **HUGE** HELP, IF THEY HELP IN THE RIGHT WAY. ADULTS WHO HELP IN THE RIGHT WAY WILL TAKE YOUR PROBLEM SERIOUSLY, WILL LISTEN AND UNDERSTAND WHAT YOU ARE GOING THROUGH, AND WILL WORK WITH YOU TO CREATE A PLAN TO SOLVE THE PROBLEM.

THE IMPORTANT THING IS THAT ALTHOUGH YOUR HELPER IS AN ADULT, THE PLAN THAT YOU CREATE TO STOP THE BULLYING IS ONE THAT YOU DEVELOP TOGETHER.

YOU HAVE A SAY IN WHAT HAPPENS.

YOU AND YOUR ADULT HELPER DECIDE TOGETHER WHAT TO DO NEXT.

IF THERE IS AN ADULT YOU FEEL YOU CAN TRUST BUT ARE NOT SURE IF HE OR SHE WILL HELP IN THE RIGHT WAY, YOU CAN ACTUALLY **TRAIN YOUR ADULT HELPER** ON HOW TO HELP YOU. THE NEXT SECTION OF THIS GUIDE, **"TRAINING YOUR ADULT HELPER,"** CAN SHOW AN ADULT EXACTLY HOW TO HELP. READ THAT SECTION WITH THE ADULT THAT YOU TRUST. THEN ASK THE ADULT HOW HE OR SHE WOULD HELP A PERSON BEING BULLIED. WOULD THE ADULT TAKE ACTION WITHOUT TALKING TO YOU FIRST? OR WOULD THE ADULT HELP YOU CREATE A PLAN THAT YOU EXECUTE TOGETHER?

IF YOU FEEL COMFORTABLE WITH THE ANSWERS, YOU HAVE FOUND YOUR ADULT HELPER. IF NOT, YOU SHOULD FIND ANOTHER ADULT. AND IF YOU GOT THIS GUIDE FROM YOUR SCHOOL, THE TEACHERS AND ADMINISTRATORS MAY HAVE ALREADY BEEN TRAINED ON HOW TO PROVIDE HELP THE RIGHT WAY.

A PLAN TO STOP BULLYING CAN BE SIMPLE. FIRST, YOU CAN BOTH READ THE SECTION **"BULLYING BASICS"** AND THEN DISCUSS HOW YOU ARE BEING BULLIED. HAVING SOMEONE TO DISCUSS IT WITH CAN HELP YOU SEE YOUR BULLYING PROBLEM DIFFERENTLY, MORE CLEARLY. SECOND, YOU CAN CONFIRM YOUR UNDERSTANDING THAT THE BULLYING IS NOT YOUR FAULT AND YOU ARE NOT FLAWED. THEN YOU CAN DECIDE WHAT YOUR NEXT ACTION WILL BE. DO YOU WANT TO TRY TO STOP THE BULLYING YOURSELF USING THE INTERACTION SKILLS THAT CAN MAKE AGGRESSION INEFFECTIVE? IF SO, READ THE SECTION **"HOW TO BULLYPROOF YOURSELF"** WITH THE ADULT TO SEE IF YOU CAN TRY ANY SKILLS THAT MIGHT MAKE SENSE FOR YOUR BULLYING SITUATION.

THE ADULT ALSO MIGHT HAVE SOME GOOD SUGGESTIONS, SUCH AS GETTING INVOLVED IN ACTIVITIES WHERE YOU CAN MAKE NEW FRIENDS. OR PERHAPS YOU'D LIKE THE ADULT TO HAVE A CONVERSATION WITH THE AGGRESSOR TO ASK THE AGGRESSOR TO STOP. THIS DOES **NOT** MEAN THE AGGRESSOR WILL GET IN TROUBLE; IT WOULD JUST BE A FRIENDLY CHAT TO ASK THE AGGRESSOR TO STOP. OR THE BULLYING MIGHT BE GETTING TO BE TOO MUCH, MORE THAN YOU CAN HANDLE, AND YOU MIGHT WANT THE ADULT TO GET THE BULLYING TO STOP. IT'S UP TO YOU. IT'S A PLAN YOU'VE HELPED CREATE.

TRAINING YOUR ADULT HELPER

> SIT, DAD! NOW ROLL OVER!

> GETTING ADULT HELP CAN BE ONE OF THE MOST EFFECTIVE WAYS TO GET BULLYING TO STOP.

IF THE BULLYING GETS REALLY BAD, IT'S BEST TO HAVE AN ADULT ON YOUR SIDE.

> PARENTS AND TEACHERS WANT TO STOP BULLYING. BUT SOMETIMES THEY AREN'T AWARE IT IS HAPPENING, EVEN IF THEY SEE THE AGGRESSIVE BEHAVIOR. YOU NEED TO TELL THEM!

> TALKING WITH AN ADULT CAN MAKE YOU FEEL BETTER, YOU CAN BOTH TALK ABOUT WHAT TO DO, AND THE ADULT CAN TAKE ACTION IF NECESSARY.

> HOWEVER, YOU MAY ACTUALLY NEED TO TRAIN YOUR ADULT HELPER! SOME ADULTS HAVE NO IDEA WHAT TO DO, AND THEY MAY GIVE YOU BAD ADVICE.

> BUT IT DOESN'T MEAN THE ADULTS DON'T CARE OR THAT YOUR PROBLEM IS NOT IMPORTANT!

> YOU CAN TRAIN AN ADULT HELPER YOURSELF. JUST READ THE NEXT SECTION TOGETHER.

> OKAY, DAD, NOW SHAKE!

HEY, ADULT!

IF A YOUNG PERSON HAS JUST PRESENTED YOU WITH THIS BOOK, THIS PERSON HAS A PROBLEM AND NEEDS YOUR HELP. PLEASE PLEASE PLEASE SIT WITH THIS PERSON AND READ THIS SECTION. THIS PERSON NEEDS YOUR SUPPORT, AND THE NEXT FEW PAGES WILL TELL YOU HOW YOU CAN DO IT. ARE YOU SITTING WITH THE PERSON IN A QUIET ROOM WITH NO DISTRACTIONS?

IF SO, PLEASE CONTINUE READING.

WE'RE MAX AND ZOEY, AND WE'RE HERE TO TALK ABOUT THE WRONG WAYS AND RIGHT WAYS TO HELP SOMEONE WHO IS BEING BULLIED.

HELPING SOMEONE AFFECTED BY BULLYING

Wrong Ways to Respond

IGNORE

ADULTS SOMETIMES DON'T LISTEN.

DISMISS PROBLEM AS UNIMPORTANT

IF IT ISN'T IMPORTANT, WHY WOULD WE BRING IT UP?

Right Ways to Respond

KNOW HOW WE FEEL

WE WANT ADULTS TO ACKNOWLEDGE HOW AWFUL BEING BULLIED CAN BE, WHETHER WE'RE BEING PICKED ON, INTIMIDATED, OR SAD FROM LOSING OUR FRIENDS.

LISTEN AND LEARN

WE WANT ADULTS TO LISTEN, UNDERSTAND, AND ASK QUESTIONS, NOT THINK THEY ALREADY KNOW EVERYTHING.

WE WANT THEM TO ASK US, "WHEN DOES IT HAPPEN? WHERE? HOW?"

SAY WE ARE NOT FLAWED

WE WANT THEM TO ACKNOWLEDGE THAT BEING THE TARGET OF AN AGGRESSOR ISN'T OUR FAULT AND THAT ANY CHARACTERISTIC USED BY THE AGGRESSOR IS NOT A FLAW BUT IS JUST AN EXCUSE TO BULLY.

WE WANT THEM TO ASK US WHAT WE WANT TO DO ABOUT IT RATHER THAN DOING SOMETHING ABOUT IT WITHOUT DISCUSSING IT FIRST. WE DON'T WANT ADULTS MAKING THE SITUATION WORSE.

KEEP IN MIND THAT IF AN ADULT WHO LOVES AND CARES ABOUT YOU LEARNS THAT YOU ARE BEING BULLIED, HE OR SHE WILL WANT TO KNOW EVERYTHING. SO BE AS OPEN AS YOU CAN.

BUT ADULTS, PLEASE UNDERSTAND THAT A STUDENT MAY WANT TO KEEP SOME THINGS PRIVATE.

AND DON'T FORGET TO TELL THE ADULT WHAT YOU WANT HIM OR HER TO DO, OR NOT TO DO. YOU SHOULD DEVELOP A PLAN TOGETHER.

IF YOUR ADULT HELPER IS NOT RESPONDING IN THE RIGHT WAY, YOU CAN ALWAYS FIND ANOTHER ADULT WHO WILL.

GOOD LUCK!

81

BORING ADULT STUFF

WHAT *YOU* CAN DO ABOUT BULLYING BY MAX AND ZOEY

CONCEPT AND TEXT BY ARI MAGNUSSON
ART AND LAYOUT BY GREG MARATHAS

ACKNOWLEDGMENTS

A HUGE THANKS TO **MICHELE DAVIS**, PRINCIPAL OF THE WARREN PRESCOTT K-8 SCHOOL, BOSTON PUBLIC SCHOOLS, AND **DR. DOMENIC AMARA**, FORMER ACADEMIC SUPERINTENDENT FOR MIDDLE AND K-8 SCHOOLS, BOSTON PUBLIC SCHOOLS, FOR PROVIDING THE IMPETUS TO CREATE THE *CIRCLEPOINT BULLYING PREVENTION PROGRAM*, OF WHICH THIS COMIC IS A COMPONENT; **KAREN ELIAS**, KINDERGARTEN TEACHER, BOSTON PUBLIC SCHOOLS, FOR HER INVALUABLE FEEDBACK AND INSIGHTS; AND THE **TEACHERS**, **PARENTS**, AND **STUDENTS** OF THE WARREN PRESCOTT K-8 SCHOOL IN CHARLESTOWN, MASSACHUSETTS, FOR THEIR SUPPORT IN PILOTING THIS COMIC.

A SPECIAL THANKS TO **ISRAEL C. KALMAN, MS**, A NOTED SCHOOL PSYCHOLOGIST, PSYCHOTHERAPIST, LECTURER, AUTHOR, BULLYING EXPERT, AND REVIEWER AND CRITIC OF BULLYING PREVENTION PROGRAMS, FOR HIS EARLY GUIDANCE ON VARIOUS BULLYING CONCEPTS. MANY OF THE DOMINANCE AGGRESSION INDIVIDUAL EMPOWERMENT TECHNIQUES IN THIS GUIDE ARE BASED ON THOSE CONTAINED IN HIS EXCELLENT BOOKS *BULLIES TO BUDDIES: HOW TO TURN YOUR ENEMIES INTO FRIENDS* AND *SUPER-DREN, THE DE-VICTIMIZER*.

AND AN EXTRA THANKS TO **DEREK MILLER** OF WESTWOOD, MA, FOR HIS VALUABLE FEEDBACK AND CONTINUED SUPPORT.

ABOUT THE AUTHOR

ARI MAGNUSSON IS AN INDEPENDENT BULLYING PREVENTION RESEARCHER, THE CREATOR OF THE *CIRCLEPOINT BULLYING PREVENTION PROGRAM*, AND THE AUTHOR OF TWO BULLYING-RELATED BOOKS: *UNDERSTANDING BULLYING AND WAYS TO MAKE IT STOP!*, AN EMPOWERMENT GUIDE FOR STUDENTS AND EDUCATORS, AND *BITOPIA*, A MIDDLE GRADE NOVEL NAMED ONE OF THE BEST BOOKS OF 2012 BY KIRKUS REVIEWS. HIS BOOKS HAVE BEEN USED IN SCHOOLS THROUGHOUT THE UNITED STATES.

ABOUT THE ILLUSTRATOR

GREG MARATHAS BEGAN HIS LIFE AS AN ARTIST ON HIS GRANDMOTHER'S FLOOR AT THE AGE OF SIX, CURLED UP WITH A PEN, PAPER, AND ART INSTRUCTION BOOKS. A LIFELONG CRAYOLA ADDICT, HE HAS SINCE BRANCHED OUT INTO VARIOUS DIGITAL AND TRADITIONAL ART-MAKING TECHNIQUES, THOUGH PENCILS AND CRAYONS WILL ALWAYS RETAIN A SPECIAL PLACE IN HIS HEART. HE RECEIVED HIS BFA IN ILLUSTRATION FROM LESLEY UNIVERSITY COLLEGE OF ART AND DESIGN.

LEGAL MUMBO JUMBO SECTION

ALL NAMES, PEOPLE, AND PLACES MENTIONED, DESCRIBED, AND DEPICTED IN THIS BOOK ARE FICTIONAL. ANY RESEMBLANCE TO ACTUAL NAMES, PEOPLE, AND PLACES IS ENTIRELY COINCIDENTAL.

COPYRIGHT © 2016 BY ARI MAGNUSSON
ALL RIGHTS RESERVED.

PUBLISHED BY
OLIVANDER PRESS LLC
BOSTON, MASSACHUSETTS
OLIVANDER, OLIVANDER PRESS, CIRCLEPOINT,
CIRCLEPOINT BULLYING PREVENTION PROGRAM,
AND ASSOCIATED LOGOS ARE TRADEMARKS OF OLIVANDER PRESS LLC.

NO PART OF THIS BOOK MAY BE REPRODUCED IN ANY FORM BY ANY MEANS WITHOUT WRITTEN PERMISSION OF THE PUBLISHER. PERMISSION IS NEVER GRANTED FOR COMMERCIAL PURPOSES. FOR INFORMATION OR TO MAKE A REQUEST REGARDING PERMISSIONS, PLEASE CONTACT OLIVANDER PRESS VIA THE CIRCLEPOINT PROGRAM WEBSITE, WWW.CIRCLEPOINTPROGRAM.ORG.

RETAIL PAPERBACK ISBN-13: 978-0-9970221-3-1
SCHOOL PAPERBACK ISBN-13: 978-0-9970221-4-8
EBOOK ISBN: 978-0-9970221-5-5

FIRST EDITION—MAY 2016

PRINTED IN THE UNITED STATES OF AMERICA

COVER AND ALL IMAGES COPYRIGHT © 2016 BY ARI MAGNUSSON

MORE INFORMATION

THIS COMIC IS A COMPONENT OF THE *CIRCLEPOINT BULLYING PREVENTION PROGRAM*, A COMPREHENSIVE PROGRAM FOR SCHOOLS AND ORGANIZATIONS THAT EMPOWERS ALL COMMUNITY MEMBERS WITH ROLE-APPROPRIATE ACTIONS AND STRATEGIES TO PREVENT, REDUCE, AND STOP BULLYING THAT WORK AT THE INDIVIDUAL, PEER GROUP, ORGANIZATION, AND COMMUNITY LEVELS. FOR MORE INFORMATION ON THE PROGRAM AND MATERIALS, INCLUDING A FREE BULLYING PREVENTION GUIDE FOR PARENTS, PLEASE VISIT THE CIRCLEPOINT PROGRAM WEBSITE.

WWW.CIRCLEPOINTPROGRAM.ORG

CENTRAL ARKANSAS LIBRARY SYSTEM
CHILDREN'S LIBRARY
LITTLE ROCK, ARKANSAS

CPSIA information can be obtained
at www.ICGtesting.com
Printed in the USA
LVOW04s1550020616

490960LV00016B/725/P